Sapa, Apa, Mana
or
Who, What, Where

Buku 1

Book 1 - Interrogatory - Part I

Chakapan Baba Ni Ari series

Baba Malay Today series

All Rights Reserved.
No part of this publication may be reproduced, stored in a retrieval system, or transmitted, in any form or by any means electronic, mechanical, photocopying, recording or otherwise, without the prior written permission of the publishers.

Theresa Fuller asserts the moral right to be identified as the author of this work.

Bare Bear Media

ISBN 978-1-925748-12-3 - Print
ISBN 978-1-925748-13-0 - Ebook

Cover by Helzkat Designs

Copyright September 2022©

Sincere thanks to my husband, Paul, who supported this work in every way possible. I love you.

National Library of Australia
US Library of Congress - TXu 2-335-835

Published 6th of September 2022

Introduction - Interrogatory Part I

Language is powerful.

In writing this text, I applied the SHOW don't TELL method. I wanted the reader to be able to pick up this book and begin to learn. Much as you would pick up a game and play.

>Chobak.
>
>To try.

The only rule in Baba Malay I wish to expound is this:

>Subject + Verb + (+ Object) + Question Word
>
>or
>
>Question Word + Subject + Verb (+ Object)

At the end of the day, have fun.

This is Baba Malay, the language of the Peranakans.

>**YOUR** language.

Baba Malay

Baba Malay is the language of my ancestors.

A language that I discovered late in 2021 was about to go extinct with fewer than a thousand speakers in the world. I took a course in Baba Malay taught by Kenneth Chan, author of *BABA MALAY FOR EVERYONE - A comprehensive guide to the Peranakan language*. This was my start to saving Baba Malay.

But I believed much more had to be done.

The book you hold in your hands is the result of my mad persistence to save my language. While there are books out there on Baba Malay, I found little in the way for children. As a teacher, I believe that to save a language we must start with the young.

I wanted a book that parents could give to their children.
One I could give to my kids.

This is my attempt.

Theresa, affectionately known in the Peranakan community as Bibek Theresa.

    Sydney,
    29th of May, 2022

Chobak

Chobak = To Try

Contents

Introduction	3
Baba Malay	4
Apa - What	8
Sapa - Who	10
Chobak - Apa/Sapa/Ni/Tu	12
Mana - Where	14
Chobak - Apa/Sapa/Mana/Ni/Tu	16
Chobak - Apa/Sapa/Mana/Ni/Tu/Gua/Gua Mia	17
Apa - What is your name?	18
Apa - Using Gua Mia	19
Bukan - Not	20
Chobak - Bukan	21
Pronouns	22
Chobak Pronouns	23
This, These, That, Those	24
Chobak - This, These, That, Those	25
Forms of Questions in English	26
Final Challenge	28
Notes	29
About the Author	30
More books in the Baba Malay Today Series	32

APA - What?

Bunga = Flower

Apa ni?
What is this?

Ni bunga.
This is a flower.

Apa tu?
What is that?

Tu bunga.
That is a flower.

Glossary

Apa = What
Bunga = Flower
Ini/ni = This
Itu/tu = That

(Ni tends to be preferred rather than ini. And tu rather than itu)

APA - What?

Tree = Pokok

Apa ni?
What is this?

Ni pokok.
This is a tree.

Apa tu?
What is that?

Tu pokok.
That is a tree.

Glossary

Apa = What
Pokok = Tree/Plant
Ini/ni = This
Itu/tu = That

(Words such as 'is' or 'are' are inferred)

SAPA - Who?

Ben

Sapa ni? or Ni sapa?
Who is this?

Ni Ben
This is Ben.

Sapa tu? Or Tu Sapa?
Who is that?

Tu Ben.
That is Ben.

Gua Ben.
I am Ben.

Glossary

Chakapan Baba = Baba Malay (the language)
Sapa = Who
Gua = I

(Sapa rather than siapa tends to be preferred usage.)

Gua mo belajair Chakapan Baba.

SAPA - Who?

Irene

Sapa ni? Or Ni sapa?
Who is this?

Ni Irene.
This is Irene.

Sapa tu? Or Tu Sapa?
Who is that?

Tu Irene.
That is Irene.

Gua Irene. Gua mia nama Irene.
I am Irene. My name is Irene.

Glossary

Gua = I
Gua mia = My
Mia/Nia = Short form of punya which indicates ownership
Nama = Name

CHOBAK - APA/SAPA/NI/TU

Cake = Kueh

Select the correct word

This is who? or Who is this?
e.g. (**Ni**/Tu) Sapa

1. What is this?
   (Apa/Sapa) ni?

2. What is that?
   (Apa/Sapa) tu?

3. This is a cake.
   (Ni/Tu) kueh.

4. That is a cake.
   (Ni/Tu) kueh.

5. The cake belongs to Ben.
   Ben (gua/mia) kueh.

6. Whose cake is this?
   (Apa/Sapa) mia kueh ni?

Answers: 1. Apa. 2. Apa. 3. Ni. 4. Tu. 5. Mia. 6. Sapa.

Lu mo belajair Chakapan Baba.

CHOBAK - APA/SAPA/NI/TU

Bird = Burong/Burung

Select the correct word

1. What is this?
   (Apa/Sapa) ni?

2. What is that?
   (Apa/Sapa) tu?

3. This is a bird.
   (Ni/Tu) burong.

4. That is a bird.
   (Ni/Tu) burong.

5. What is that?
   Apa (ni/tu)?

6. What is this?
   Apa (ni/tu)?

Answers: 1. Apa. 2. Apa. 3. Ni. 4. Tu. 5. Tu. 6. Ni.

MANA - Where?

Bird = Burong

Garden = Kebun

Mana burong?
Where is the bird?

Burong dalam kebun.
The bird is in the garden.

Mana burong pi?
Where has the bird gone?

Burong pi dalam kebun.
The bird has gone into the garden.

Glossary

Burong/Burung = Bird
Dalam = In
Kebun = Garden
Mana = Where
Pi = Go

Gua mo belajair Chakapan Baba.

MANA - Where?

Cake = Kueh

Apa ni?
What is this?

Ni kueh.
This is a cake.

Mana kueh?
Where is the cake?

Kueh kat atair meja.
The cake is on the table.

Sapa mia kueh ni? Or Ni kueh sapa mia? Ni gua mia kueh.
Whose cake is this? This is my cake.

(Although 'mia' sounds like the Hokkien word for name, the word 'mia' or 'nia' is actually derived from the word 'punya' meaning ownership.)

    Glossary
Atair = Top
Gua mia = My, Lu Mia = Your, Sapa Mia = Whose
Kat = On
Kueh = Cake, Meja = Table

CHOBAK - APA/SAPA/MANA/NI/TU

Ben
Translate into Baba Malay

1. Gua mia nama Ben.
2. Gua orang Peranakan. Or Gua Peranakan.
3. Gua pi kebun.
4. Mana Ben?
5. Ben pi mana?

Answers: 1. My name is Ben. 2. I am Peranakan. 3. I go to the garden. 4. Where is Ben? 5. Where has Ben gone? Or Ben has gone where?

CHALLENGE! Answer these questions

1. Sapa tu?
2. Mana Ben pi?
3. Ben orang apa?

Answers: 1. That is Ben. Tu Ben. 2. Ben went to the garden. Ben pi kebun. 3. Ben is Peranakan. Ben orang Peranakan.

Glossary

Orang = People, Orang Peranakan = Peranakan, Nama = Name

Jorang mo belajair Baba Malay.

CHOBAK - APA/SAPA/MANA/NI/TU/GUA/GUA MIA

Irene

Select the correct word

1. Who is this?
   (Sapa/Mana) ni?

2. Who is that?
   (Apa/Sapa) tu?

3. My name is Irene.
   (Gua/Gua mia) nama Irene.

4. I am a Peranakan.
   Gua (Orang China/Orang Peranakan.)

5. Where is Irene?
   (Apa/Sapa/Mana) Irene?

6. I am Irene.
   (Gua/Gua mia) Irene.

> Glossary
> Orang China = Chinese,   Orang Peranakan = Peranakan

Answers: 1. Sapa. 2. Sapa. 3. Gua mia. 4. Orang Peranakan. 5. Mana. 6. Gua.

APA - What is your name?

Irene

Apa lu mia nama? Or
Lu mia nama apa? Or
Lu punya nama apa?
What is your name?

Gua mia nama Irene.
My name is Irene.

Nama lu punya apa?
What is your name?

Apa dia mia nama?
What is her/his name?

Glossary

Apa = What
Dia = He/She
Dia mia = His/her
Gua = I
Gua mia = My
Lu = You,   Lu punya = Your,   Lupa = Forget
Nama = Name

Chakapan Baba lu punya chakapan.

APA - Using Gua Mia

Cat = Kuching

Ini kuching sapa mia?
Literally translated as 'This cat is whose?' ie., Whose cat is this?

Itu kuching sapa mia?
That cat is whose?

Sapa mia kuching ni?
Whose cat is this?

Kuching ni gua mia.
This is my cat.

Gua lupa ni kuching lu mia.
I forget this cat is yours.

Ni lu mia kuching.
This is your cat.

(The word 'mia' is used to indicate possession.)

BUKAN - Not

Flower = Bunga

Ni bunga bukan gua mia.
This flower is not mine.

Ni bunga bukan lu mia.
This flower is not yours.

Ni bunga bukan Ben mia.
This flower is not Ben's.

Ni bunga bukan Irene mia bunga.
This flower is not Irene's flower.

Ni bunga bukan pokok.
This flower is not a tree.

Itu bunga bukan lu mia bunga.
That flower is not your flower.

Tu buku bukan bunga.
That is a book not a flower.

> Glossary
> Buku = Book
> Mo = Want

CHOBAK - BUKAN

Tree = Pokok
Translate into English

1. Ni bukan bunga. Ni pokok.

2. Tu pokok bukan bunga.

3. Ni pokok bukan Ben mia.

4. Ni bukan bunga. Ni bukan pokok.

5. Ni bukan Ben. Ni bukan Irene.

6. Ni Ben bukan Irene.

7. Itu buku. Bukan Bunga. Bukan pokok.

Answers: 1. This is not a flower. This is a tree. 2. That tree is not a flower. 3. This tree is not Ben's. Or This tree does not belong to Ben. 4. This is not a flower. This is not a tree. 5. This is not Ben. This is not Irene. 6. This is Ben not Irene. 7. That is a book. Not a flower. Not a tree.

PRONOUNS

Gua = I (This is the familiar form of salutation)
Saya = I (This is the polite form)

Lu = you
Lu (plural) = Lorang, or Lu orang = All of you

Dia = He/She

(Always look at the context.)

They = Jorang, Dia Orang, Diorang

We = Kita

Examples:

Gua Ben.
I am Ben.

Lu Irene.
You are Irene.

Saya Irene.
I am Irene.

Dia Ben. Dia Irene.
He is Ben. She is Irene.

Lorang chakap chakapan Baba.
You all speak Baba Malay. or All of you speak Baba Malay.

CHOBAK PRONOUNS

Ben

Irene

Translate into English

1. Gua bukan Ben. Gua Irene.

2. Saya Irene bukan Ben.

3. Ben bukan Irene.

4. Kita orang Peranakan. Or Kita Peranakan.

5. Lorang orang Peranakan. Or Lu orang Peranakan.

6. Dia Ben. Dia bukan Irene.

7. Jorang ni orang Peranakan.

8. Dia bukan Ben. Dia Irene.

Answers: 1. I am not Ben. I am Irene. 2. I am Irene not Ben. 3. Ben is not Irene. 4. We are Peranakan. 5. All of you are Peranakan. 6. He is Ben. He is not Irene. 7. They over here are Peranakan. 8. She is not Ben. She is Irene.

THIS. THESE, THAT, and THOSE

This = Ini or Ni
These = Ini or Ni
That = Itu or Tu
Those = Itu or Tu

Examples:

Ini pokok.
This is a tree.

Itu pokok.
That is a tree.

Ini pokok-pokok.
These are trees.

Itu pokok-pokok.
Those are trees.

Tree = Pokok

Glossary

Cake = Kueh
Cakes = Kueh-kueh
Chocolate = Chocolate
Sayang = Love
Suka = Like
Pokok = Tree
Pokok-pokok = Trees

Garden = Kebun

(We can repeat some words to indicate plural or else use 'ramay' or 'manyak' which is beyond the scope of this beginner's book.)

CHOBAK THIS, THESE, THAT, and THOSE

Cake = Kueh

Translate into Baba Malay or English

1. That is a cake.

2. These are cakes.

3. Those are cakes.

4. This is not a cake.

5. This is not a chocolate cake. (Hint: Adjectives come after nouns.)

6. Ni kueh-kueh.

7. Itu kueh-kueh.

8. Tu kueh.

Answers: 1. Tu kueh. 2. Ni kueh-kueh. 3. Itu kueh-kueh. 4. Ni bukan kueh. 5. Ni bukan kueh chocolate. 6. These are cakes. 7. Those are cakes. 8. That is a cake.

Forms of Questions in English

In English there are many ways of asking questions. Not all question words, however, have their Baba Malay equivalent.

Are = No Baba Malay equivalent
Can = Boleh
Could = Boleh
Do = No Baba Malay equivalent
Did = No Baba Malay equivalent
Have = Ada
How = Apa Macham or Amcham (Description)
Is = No Baba Malay equivalent
Was = No Baba Malay equivalent
Were = No Baba Malay equivalent
What = Apa
When = Bila
Where = Mana
Why = Apasair or apasal or kenapa
Will = Boleh

Examples:

Are you coming?
Lu mo datang?

Can you come?
Literally translated as 'Boleh lu datang?' but 'Lu boleh datang?' is also used.

Could you come?
Boleh lu datang?

Do you want to come?
Lu mo datang?

Did you want to come?
Lu mo datang?

Have you any flowers?
Lu ada bunga?

How is your bird?
Apa macham lu mia burung?

Is this a flower?
Ni bunga?

Was this your flower?
Ni lu mia bunga?

Were these your flowers? (NOTE: Bunga can mean flower or flowers.)
Ini lu mia bunga?

What is that?
Apa tu?

When are you coming?
Bila lu datang?

Where are your flowers?
Mana lu mia bunga?

Why are you coming?
Apasair lu datang? Or Apasal lu datang. Or Kenapa lu datang?

Will you come?
Boleh lu datang? Or Lu Boleh datang?

Glossary
Datang = Come or Coming

FINAL CHALLENGE

Translate into Baba Malay the following sentences:

1. I am Irene.

2. This is my flower.

3. This is a garden.

4. My name is Ben.

5. This is my cat.

6. Those are trees.

7. I am Peranakan.

8. You are Peranakan.

9. We are not Peranakan.

10. What is your name?

11. Who are you?

12. Where is she?

Answers: 1. Gua Irene. 2. Ni gua mia bunga. 3. Ni kebun. 4. Gua mia nama Ben. 5. Ni gua mia kuching. 6. Tu pokok-pokok. 7. Gua orang Peranakan. 8. Lu orang Peranakan. 9. Kita bukan orang Peranakan. 10. Apa lu mia nama? 11. Sapa lu? 12. Mana dia?

Now it's *your* turn

NOTES

Baba Malay or Chakapan Baba or the Baba language was born when Chinese traders sailed down to Southeast Asia and intermarried with the local women. A mix of Hokkien and Malay, Baba Malay went into decline after WWII as many Peranakans were killed.

This is the reason why there are no Baba Malay equivalent to some words today. When in doubt English words are often used.

Another reason is language assimilation.

There are also two registers to Baba Malay:

1. Alus i.e., a refined form that women tended to speak.
2. Kasair i.e., a coarser version practised by men.

Baba Malay tended to be spoken rather than written so there are many variations in the spelling e.g.,

kreja or kerja (work)

When in doubt I referred to Kenneth Chan's *Baba Malay For Everyone - A comprehensive guide to the Peranakan language* as well as William Gwee Thian Hock's *A Baba Malay Dictionary.*

Baba Malay is also sadly considered an endangered language.

Let's do our best to change this!

Bibek Theresa

About the Author

Theresa Fuller

Theresa Fuller has always loved stories and story-telling, but it was not until the birth of her first son that she became a full-time writer. Her aim was to write stories about her culture: Southeast Asia.

Theresa was Head of Computing at various private schools in Sydney. She has also been a Higher School Certificate (HSC) Examiner and HSC Assessor. Her teaching degrees have seen her work in primary and secondary schools and at Kalgoorlie College in Western Australia.

Her first published novel in 2018 was THE GHOST ENGINE, a steampunk fantasy about the fictitious granddaughter of Ada Lovelace, the world's first programmer. Theresa has published books on Southeast Asian mythology: THE GIRL WHO BECAME A GODDESS (2019), THE GIRL SUDAN PAINTED LIKE A GOLD RING (2022) and EATING THE LIVER OF THE EARTH - collection of the lost folktales of the mousedeer Sang Kanchel.

In 2023, WHERE CRANES WEAVE AND BAMBOO SINGS a visual narrative textbook for children and beginner writers was published.

In 2020, Theresa lost many family members. She threw heself into researching her family history as a way to deal with her grief. This was when she discovered that the language of her ancestors - Baba Malay - was on the verge of extinction. As a writer, teacher and selfpublishing author, Theresa found herself in an unusual position - she was able to create the curriculum that was needed to help fill a vacuum.

The result is the **Baba Malay Today** series. And now the **New Peranakan Tales** series starting with GUA PI KEDAY.

All in aid of saving the language.

www.theresafuller.com

Thank you for your support!

More Books in the Baba Malay Today Series

Book 1 - Interrogatory Part I   SAPA, APA, MANA or
                                     WHO, WHAT, WHERE

Book 2 - Interrogatory Part II   AMCHAM, APASAIR, BILA or
                                     HOW, WHY, WHEN

Book 3 - Conjunctions   TAPI, ABIS, PASAIR or
                                     BUT, SO, BECAUSE

Book 4 - Prepositions   ATAIR, KAT, BAWAH or
                                     TOP, NEAR, BOTTOM

Book 5 - Antonyms   ALUS, KA, KASAR or
                                     DELICATE, OR, COARSE

Book 6 - Essence   CHAKAPAN BABA ATI or
                                     THE HEART OF BABA MALAY

Book 7 - Poetry   CHAKAPAN BABA PANTON or
                                     BABA MALAY POETRY

Book 8 - Idioms   CHAKAPAN BABA CHAKAPAN or
                                     BABA MALAY IDIOMS

Dear Reader,

Thank you for the purchase of this book.

Please help us spread the word as we try to save our language.

Bibek Theresa

Sydney, 18th of June, 2022

Jangan lupakan Chakapan Baba.

www.ingramcontent.com/pod-product-compliance
Lightning Source LLC
Chambersburg PA
CBHW070341120526
44590CB00017B/2982